RETURNING

TO *Love*

LONDYN MICHAELE

RETURNING TO LOVE

All rights reserved. For announcements, special free content, limited-edition releases, and an all-around good read, join our mailing list!

To do so, visit: www.lovereinterpreted.com

Follow us on Instagram: @Lovereinterpreted

Watch me on Youtube: Lovereinterpreted

First Edition: 2020

Printed in the United States of America

Paperback ISBN: 978-1-7358496-0-7

eBook ISBN: 978-1-7358496-1-4

Illustration Designs by Kailaiillustration

Website: (www.kailai.co.uk)

Instagram: @Kailaiillustration

Just for you.

This is for everyone who has ever hesitated to take a chance on love.

You deserve it.

CONTENTS

RETURNING

TO *Love*

LOVE DEFINED

SOUTHERN HOSPITALITY

Your love always feels like home to me.

LILIES

Our love is complex in its own way.
It has created a newness inside of me and you.
How you present your love to me,
not clothed with perfection but gentle, pure,
intentional.
All the things I daydream about,
love is no longer one of my coffee shop thoughts,
It's our reality.
I'm scared to share it with someone else.
Because for however long,
this feeling continues to reside inside of me.
Like a well-watered plant,
I want to protect it from harmful things,
But it needs the sunlight to breathe and you –
attending to my needs,
replenishing the soil,
removing the dead pieces.
Watching me bloom,
watering me every day,
careful not to oversaturate.
Giving me just enough space and time to grow.
Then, repeating.

90's R&B

The way that I love you,
Feels like my favorite song on repeat.
I close my eyes
and
imagine you here lying next to me.
I get lost in the words, the rhythm, the beat.
I replay this scene again
and
again.
It will never get old to me.
When I find myself wanting you,
I quietly hum the tune.
I can't recreate this moment or feeling
with anyone but you.
You are my song.

JOHN COLTRANE

It's been months since I last saw you,
Six, to be exact.
But I remember the smallest things so vividly.
I still feel your embrace when you hug me,
– your fingertips tracing the small of my back.
How you like the fan blowing loudly
And the shadows of your frame bouncing off the
walls of white.
Lemon pepper wings,
And whiskied Friday nights.
My favorite "smallest thing", your eye contact.
Your laugh channels this cosmic energy inside of
me.
This evening we have a date at 7:30,
Well maybe that's not what we want to call it.
My palms are sweaty,
And butterflies slow dance in the bottom of my
stomach.
I think of how I think of kissing you,
every time you're close to me.
Maybe it was space much needed.
One thing I've learned recently,
if love lights the way,
don't run from it,
Lead it.

NEW BIRTH

Cleansed with your thoughts,
birthed with your words.
Finding a way to describe this,
is it a noun or a verb?
There's no formality,
or perfect script,
I love you.
Every day I crave to hear it,
sounds the best,
departing from your rounded lips.

LOVE SOUNDS

If our love was a soundtrack,
I'd want the perfect intro.
Not too deep,
Instead, easing into the melody,
To a slow beat.
Drums met with bass,
Highs and lows,
Soft vocals at the perfect tone.
No songs skipped,
One note intertwining with the next.
Yeah, I think I like that.
As the songs play,
I feel like I've lost track of time.
for the last two hours,
I feel like I'm stuck in a daze.
I can't remember every word,
but the new memories,
stay on replay.
A love that leaves me speechless,
Vivid thoughts in stereo,
Left with pen and notebook,
written words,
I won't let go.

JUST THINKING

I think of you when the sun rises.
I think of you when the sun sets.
The place where our hearts met.
Truth is,
I'm always thinking of you.

KEYS TO THE CITY

The way my tongue spoke to your body,
I was loving you in metaphors.
If I unlocked the key to your heart,
I knew it was so much more.
Door after door,
You've opened up to me.
Now I can say I know the real you,
and all that you bring.
You are a light, a presence, a gift to me.
Thank God for entrusting me with your heart,
and
presenting me with the key.

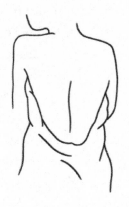

JULY

Summer breezes,
like the kinds that run over my toes,
between the sheets.
I don't want to get up,
under hypnosis,
with your every touch
On point.

AM OR PM

What if I told you I loved you?
Would that scare you off or be too much?
I've been wanting to utter those three words,
for months.
Yet, they sit they're lodged in the back of my throat.

Should I tell you when I first wake up?
Three unfiltered words would be the first thing you
would hear.
A beautiful way to begin your day.
Dawn, breaking,
Sunlight creeping through the windows,
The birds, beginning to sing.
Or after we have dinner?
Glasses of wine in hand,
two-stepping in the living room,
dancing to Harold Melvin sing them blue notes.

We are day and night,
So I'm sure you'd prefer the p.m.
I may not have the owner's manual,
this requires something totally different.
I can feel it.
So I proceed with caution,
As I say I love you,
Rare. Irreplaceable. Midday edition.

COCOA BUTTER KISSES

Let's just skip all the small talk.
I want you for breakfast, lunch, dinner
and
everything in between.
Something about that,
just feels right to me.
A hint of cocoa butter scented kisses,
painting my love with your fingertips.
The space between your lips,
Is what my body craves.
Just being in your presence,
I know it's only a matter of time,
Before I misbehave.

A TOAST

Let's celebrate,
me and you.
How one became two,
Surprisingly my heart is at ease.
I can't believe it.
Cheers to our love.

AMOR, AMOUR

Love language unknown,
But let me interpret.
Holding you near,
I can feel it.
Deep in my veins,
I'm breaking out like Bruce Banner,
I can't hold back.
The Incredible Hulk is screaming inside of me.
Two-stepping,
maintaining a safe distance.
With you,
it feels so easy,
I want you to trust me,
like you trust your spirit.
Careful to pronounce every consonant and vowel.
I'm totally content with this right now.
Mi amor mixed with a little *oui oui*.
It really doesn't matter,
let me translate.
Looking deeply into your eyes,
I see pieces of me in your reflection.
Let me inside those innermost parts,
deep inside your mind,
that you try so hard to escape from.
Captivated by your words,
Despite not knowing what any of them mean.

BLUE WATERS

Love like the river,
flowing from my heart to yours.
Gentle.

SOMETHING NEW

Got my attention,
It's undivided.
I'm all ears,
ready to listen.
As you pour out your heart,
joys and fears,
holding mine in contentment.
I'm connected to you in ways
I've never experienced.
Let's not let this moment fade,
timeless interaction.

EIGHTY-NINE
CONSTELLATIONS

Maybe I'll be as lucky as you,
As the sun and earth collide.
The clouds exchange kisses,
underneath the moonlight,
Miami nights.

The magnetic energy pulls them closer,
A hypnotizing fragrance.
at that very moment,
The two become entangled.

I'll be wishing upon a star
I've named it David.
Far apart from the rest,
in a world of its own,
The 89th constellation.
I know my wishes will come true,
I visualized this years ago,
love without reservations.

ENGLISH AS
SECOND LANGUAGE

See love is my first language,
English as a second,
forming syllables and consonants.
Passing with flying colors.
I hold you in high regard as my dictionary,
defined by no other.
Excuse me if I don't pronounce this correctly in
English,
I'm lost in love's transitions.
Wading in your presence,
waiting for your blessing.
Now let's move forward,
I've mastered this language.
Love is my first,
English is my second.

TAKING CHANCES

All too many times,
you were focused on what love was not.
When I just wanted to show you,
What love could truly be.
Parallels of space between the two,
defined galaxies of love,
brand new.

WHISPERS IN THE DARK

You asked me why my eyes were closed.
I quietly whispered,
Thank you God.

ARRHYTHMIA

My heart beats for you in ways
my speech
could never articulate.

SOMETHING TO WRITE
HOME ABOUT

Ooh mama,
I can't wait til' you meet her.
She is beautiful.
The kind you walk by and stare in awe at.
Her skin glows like it was birthed at sunset.
Voice soft like melons,
Strong and courageous.
This is the kind of woman,
I've dreamed about for a long time.
Glad I didn't settle for the easy ones.
Willing to work for her love,
She sits among the queens.
She deserves petals to be thrown at her feet,
adorned with kisses and hugs.
Mama,
This is the one who helped me define love.
Holding her heart,
As if it was my own.
Would it be wrong to feel like,
forever is too short?

HALF AND HALF

I loved mornings with you.
The sound of the blaring alarm,
Your body scooting closer,
Holding me tight.
Hitting snooze to get five more minutes of sleep.
It was in those quiet moments,
I loved us most.
Not a word spoken,
with every breath you became part of me.
Waking up to make your coffee,
Just the way you liked,
Half a cup,
but mostly filled with cream.
Met with a soft kiss that said,
"Have a good day, I can't wait to get back to you"
and all the things in between.
Today you are the reason,
I prefer my cup black, no sugar, no cream.

SUNSET

Your love reminds me of the sun,
Peaking behind the clouds.
I knew it was there,
But wasn't ready to shine yet.
It didn't matter to me.
I stood right beside you.
Hand in hand,
Watching it grow,
Patiently waiting
Like I wait for the sunset.

ME & YOU

You couldn't piece your words together.
Your tongue and mouth battled against each other,
like David and Goliath,
Fighting each other for room.
I studied you every day so when I spoke,
We became one in sync and tune.
I am here consoling you,
while you heal from old wounds.
When I say I love you,
I mean it deeply,
like a mother connected to her unborn child in the
womb.
When you stare me in my eyes,
and hold me for hours,
I find myself rendered speechless,
imitating your moves.
But I am also content,
because I am happy and freely lost in love,
with all of you.

REVELATIONS

In the end,
Just like the beginning.
I wanted it to be you.
I have never been so sure of anything,
Not even myself.
Timeless interactions,
Never love subtracted.
I am convinced,
I was created solely for you.
I always thought it sounded silly,
For someone to say that
"You're my person".
Maybe because I hadn't found it yet,
better yet allow it to find me.
Or perhaps I secretly longed for it deep within.
I'm not sure how it happened,
but I found myself under your spell.
Ain't no abracadabra or made-up fantasies,
what we share is beyond insanity.
Scared,
Yet willing to yield to our imperfections,
As long as you're next to me.

UNRAVELED

CHANGES IN THE WEATHER

Storms or clouds,
with you I could never really tell the difference.
No alarms to warn me of the hurt,
time wasted,
that could have been prevented.
Energy misplaced,
Stuck living with the consequences of my poor
decisions.
Once lighting struck,
the sky lit up.
Everything suddenly made sense,
And we soon ended.

GRAY AREA

Soft love.
Hard love.
Blurry lines.
Long nights.
Early morning.
Confused between
do you just lust after me,
Or really want me.
Text too long to read,
hearts deceived,
makes it so difficult to leave.
My heart tells me it's wrong to stay,
But my mind knows that ain't right.

PHONE HOME

Feels weird not coming home to you.
Every day I sit in front of the house.
Car parked,
silence.
I can hear all the things I never paid attention to
before.
I can hear the echo of your voice in my head.
Standing in the doorway,
eyes filled with excitement,
Perfectly painted picture.
Now I love you through a tinted glass,
I never told you.
I guess it's too late,
I wanted us forever.

DRIED TEARS

I cried so much,
there were no tears left to wipe.
Externally I smiled,
But internally, it was the fight of my life.
Stillness.
I couldn't move.
Deep breaths,
Inhaling and exhaling
is how I learned,
to self-soothe.

DON'T

I made my list of to do's,
you were not included.

LOSING BETS

Eyes watery I can't see my next step.
Gasping for air,
where I'm dependent on you for my next breath.
I breathed you deeply,
you consume all of me.
I thought I needed your love, like I depended on the
air to breathe.
But see, what I really needed was me.
The real me, to love myself, and love me from a
clear view.
a love I raised the stakes to get
That was by far my safest bet.

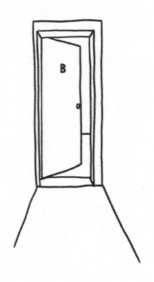

APARTMENT B

I hear you knocking,
But somehow I can't muster the courage to let you
in.
Bandages and stitches over old wounds.
Aches that seem to rear their ugly faces every now
and then.
I don't want to do this casually.
I want your love to gravitate to where mine ends.
You are my lover turned best friend.
Strings intertwined,
glasses half-filled,
with the best imported wines.

HERE WE GO AGAIN

Missing your voice,
Too bad we are worlds apart.
I listen to your voicemails from time to time.
Reminds me of the coldness in my heart.
Wishing it was different,
but I know I could never retract.
Hearts at war,
laced with fear.
Rounds fired,
like we're deployed in Iraq.
Who am I lying to?
Not sure if it's either me or you.
Truth is,
I want you.
I'd honestly rather tell you all this in person,
just thought I'd let you know.
I can't call you,
So I wrote this poem.

BLURRY VISION

Hearts broken,
I can't focus.
Recounting our last convos.
The sound of your voice,
Echoes out to me.
Shivers from the slightest little touch,
I really hate that I miss you so much.
Just move on,
Is what they say.
Maybe you've never had a love,
That would turn your brightest morning into your
darkest day.
Tick, tock.
Hoping to fast forward time.
Time heals all,
move on.
But right now it's not moving,
and I'm left in this state of shock.
I don't want to do this all by myself,
tick after lonely tock.

VOIDS

I was hoping to feel,
feel at least something.
That would take
my mind away
from the nothing I feel,
when I'm with you.

JUNKIES

Making love,
singing ballads,
let me open your pallet.
Jet setting from country to country all on one flight.
A night of ecstasy,
leaving each other high and dry,
Stuck in daydream fantasies.
Let's go.
I'm ready to explore new places.
Wherever you are, just leave right now,
I got us covered with the who, what, when and how.
Looking at my clock counting down,
waiting til you get here.
I'm looking forward to the thought of just us.
I wish I could call this love,
but truth is I know it's lust.

UNWANTED GUESTS

Why did you invite me here?
Maybe things weren't made clear between the two
of us.
Long nights,
early mornings,
intentions blurred with gray lines.
Pretty lies entrapped between your sweet lips and
mine.
Disguised with lust,
masked with fear.
It's too late now,
we're here.
I could feel myself starting to love you,
for all the wrong reasons.
Silly of me to think it would last,
but wise enough to know,
Everything has a time and a season.

PLATEAU

I knew it was a platform,
Where two could not exist.
Deep down it just felt like
butterflies in the bottom of my stomach pit.
Like the moment right before,
the first time we kissed.
I wanted to cultivate a space where both of us could
run,
wild and free in love.
Finding that balance was nerve-wrecking,
but I'm not one to back down from a challenge.
This place I spoke of,
existed in my heart and not in my mind.
As we danced around in circles, together in love,
it was only a matter of time.

SHOW AND TELL

Tell me you love me again.
More so,
Show me you love me again.
So I'll never have to hear you say it.

LITTLE WHITE LIES

I double checked my list just to be sure.
Intelligent, respectful, God fearing, centered,
silly but mature.
Checking off the positives and negatives,
The good outweighed the bad by far.
It was everything I wanted,
But I knew I wasn't ready for.

I still strung you along.
I leaped in hopes that you would catch me,
and stay along for the ride.
Maybe timing wasn't right.
Either way you definitely deserved someone willing
to put up a fight.

Easiest thing to say was "It's not you, it's me."
Nothing could be further from the truth.
Yes I know,
a cowardice move on my behalf.
Grateful for your patience,
something I could not repay.
Forever indebted,
to the love that you gave.

MUST I REMIND YOU

Your love
shouldn't have made you absent of your
responsibility.
You wanted this, remember?
You chose me.
So why is it that I need to remind you on the daily?

STARVING

Aesthetically pleasing,
Looking at a full plate.
Slow cooked,
But it's dressed with lust, lies, and selfishness.
All the things I hate.
So instead of partaking,
I remain hungry.
I refuse to eat.
I'll just sit here at this table and wait.

UNAPOLOGETIC

So many words you could've chosen from to say.
The two I never heard depart from your lips,
I'm sorry.

BUZZED

Hangover type of love,
how much did I drink?
It's 12 o'clock and I just woke up.
Did I even stop to think?
What this would do to me?
Liquor running through my blood,
Selfishly hurting others with my lack of love.
I wish I could say I was totally naïve,
But I wasn't, contrary to popular brief.

MY PLAYLIST

There were songs I wanted you to hear,
they were all about you.

NEEDS AND WANTS

Something about you needing me,
didn't sit quite right.
To need greater than the desire of want.
Like, have you really tapped into your innermost
thoughts?
Reflections of yourself,
projecting them on to others.
I'm sorry I couldn't be what you needed.
This is your final notice.
I am not your lover.
I do not want you back.

INSOMNIA

3 AM thoughts of you,
when I definitely should be sleep.
Your loving spirit always seems to creep.
Finding a way in,
to fill those cavities.
Love fulfilled at maximum capacity.
I love that even the days we are apart,
I smile, because you live inside my heart.

I JUST DIDN'T WANT
TO GO TO ARIZONA

I went on a long run today.
Started off as one, but ended up being eight.
I made a new recipe but nothing that you'd like.
I changed my sheets,
corners tightly tucked,
your side of the bed perfectly intact.
It's been some time so I finally unblocked your
number,
and
turned off the read receipts.
I called my cousins,
we hadn't talked since Christmas.
I washed the dishes that you always complained
about.
I watched Martin reruns.
So I'm sorry I lied to you.
I did all these things to avoid missing you today.

JUST MAYBE

Maybe this love isn't,
What you thought it would be.
Maybe you're scared of diving in with both eyes
open,
Cold feet.
Maybe this is not "his" story
but "her" story.
Maybe love is stronger than your greatest fears.
Maybe this turns out better than expected.
Maybe love always pays itself forward.
When you don't reject it.

PIECES

I am broken,
and cannot love you in fragments.

THIS IS ALL
NEW TO ME

PERMISSION

I am ready to love you.
And by you,
I mean me.

METAMORPHOSIS

Always,
All ways.
Your love forever resonates,
with my darkest nights,
and sunniest days.
Praying for a smile,
when I look at your face.
So I feel what it's like to get a glimpse of heaven.
Purpose by design,
God made you,
first in my eyes,
Never a second.
Placed on a pedestal,
your name rings across the skies,
with the likes of Yemaya and Oshun.
Watching you grow day by day in his image,
you transform.
So I call you my butterfly,
leaving her cocoon.

RED LIGHT,
GREEN LIGHT

Maybe we shouldn't love each other,
Because neither one of us knows how this ends.
I wish I could rewind the time.
I would have loved you sooner.
So much wasted time,
"What if's" cross my mind.
Holding back what I really want to say,
~~Fuck~~ it.
Let's love each other forever,
starting with today.

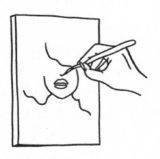

MONA LISA

My love needed a resting place.
Somewhere warm, with a roof, a cozy bed,
a place I could call home.
I was tired.
I had been homeless before,
surrounded by people that unwelcomed me.
Residing where I thought lust would turn into love.
I've been waiting to give love a new meaning.
I was giving love a beautiful beginning.
With every page turned,
every brush stroke,
the vision became clearer.
I was painting myself a new picture.

SPRING IN BLOOM

Three hundred sixty-five days later,
You are nowhere in my sight.
My mind feels clear,
and my heart feels light.
Filling myself up with love from inside out.
Layers shed,
and the best parts now in sprout.
Fear and uncertainty no longer consume me.
How beautiful is it to know that,
I am blooming.

MOUNT EVEREST

I proclaimed, *I love you,*
from the mountain tops.
To only feel echoes returned.
Seclusion.
Nomad wandering,
from heart to heart.
Loving myself is a journey,
the purest form of art.

PURPOSE DRIVEN

I want to love you on purpose.
Show me where,
show me how.
I want to love you on purpose.
Not tomorrow, right here, right now.
Tell me how it feels.
Do you want more?
Or should I hold back?
I want to love you on purpose.
Let's meet somewhere in between
and
fill each other where we lack.

PRESENTS

I know it's peace,
because every time I sit next to you,
I feel God's presence.

LOST ART

I had to lose you,
in order to get to the next level.
I found myself loving me more,
that was the best part.
The road to love ourselves is a lost art.
Forgive yourself for counting yourself out,
while adding others in.
Digging beyond the surface,
is how the journey begins.

SWEETEST LOVE

I smile at the thought of it.
Composed of genuine intentions, and fully present.
I look in the mirror and no longer have to
reminisce.
It's not empty love masked with hugs, sex, or a kiss.
I face myself because it's me,
it is who I am.
Giving myself daily deposits,
some small and some large,
depending on what my heart requires.
I never had to look for the fulfillment anywhere else,
Because I've found what my life requires.
Learning to love myself is the true meaning of
wealth.
Yes, it's me.
I am the sweetest love.
The kind you daydream about in the morning.
The light peeking through the darkness.
I didn't need validation from someone else.
I am the one who I look to when I need to be
recharged.
I'm so happy I found the sweetest love,
the sweetest love is me.

NATURALLY GIFTED

Got my attention,
it's undivided.
I'm all ears,
ready to listen.
As you pour out your heart,
joys and fears,
holding mine in contentment.
I'm connected to you in ways,
my body's never experienced.
Let's not let this moment fade,
I don't want to forget this.
I commend myself on being a fast learner.
You could say I'm naturally gifted.
It's only two months in,
and
I'm learning to speak your love language.

GOOD AND PLENTY

Everyone deserves love,
but not my kind.
You didn't deserve it.
Is that what's meant by,
love is blind?

REFRESH

You are perfect timing.
I couldn't have painted a better picture.
The deeper our love becomes,
I find myself imagining,
My first name being preceded with Mrs.

Walking hand in hand,
is not something I'm unfamiliar with,
But this love has a different type of grip.
It's an imperfect love but I cannot explain it.
I've finally met someone,
that will keep this wild thing tamed.

CONFESSIONS

Masked behind,
weaves, sew-ins and braids.
Nails a little shorter than Jackie Joyner Kersee's.
Batting my sweet long lashes,
behind my knockoff Cartier shades.
Drenched in] Fenty lip gloss.

Who's standing in front of the mirror?
Once I strip down?
I do this for me,
not for you.
Lies I tell,
just so I don't feel lost –
I find myself more me,
humbly uncovered,
beneath it all.

READY. SET. GO

I already had a head start.
With every rapid breath and every long stride.
I could feel my adrenaline rushing,
I had to pace myself.
Ready. Set. Go.
I zoned out and silenced everyone else.
From the fourth lane to the first,
I pulled my strength out of nowhere, as I was dying
of thirst.
I stepped across the finish line,
Face full of tears.
For the very first time,
I was experiencing what it felt like to put myself first
in years.

LOVE AND LIGHT

I hope that love is filling the darkest places of you
right now.
Voids that have never seen light.

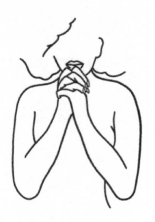

DIVINE

I thank God for many things.
One thing my prayers always have in common,
You.

NICE TO MEET YOU

The first day we met,
Before thinking of any "No's",
My heart already said yes.
Your lips were moving,
but I didn't hear anything that came out.
We exchanged nervous smiles.
In an instant, you already knew how to put my heart
at ease.
I was no longer fearful,
to see what love had to give me.

FACIAL RECOGNITION

I'm on prayer 3,052,
I've probably lost count.
Mostly filled with "thank you's"
I could never repay.
Some selfish prayers like "God bless me with this"
or "provide me with that today".
Overflowing with gratitude,
I want to cry but I can't.
Tears of joy,
I feel somewhat unworthy.
Here I am,
In front of you.
Face to face,
I look deeply in your eyes.
Dreaming with my eyes wide open.
Trying to find out if it leads me home.
You take a proud,
Yet soft glance at me.
I give you a masked smile.
I'd been caught red handed.
I'm standing, looking at reflection in the mirror.
Rest assure,
I'm prepared to love you.
Falling,
stumbling in self-love,
but ready to stand for it all.

NEW MOONS

Let's go somewhere our cell phones are out of range.
Eyes locked,
Thoughts exchanged.
Just me and you,
at the forefront of each other's mind.
Talking for hours,
losing track of time.
Telling stories we'll vaguely remember.
Gazing into the darkness,
as stars light up the summer sky.
Giggling at the smallest things,
none of it makes sense.
Who would have ever thought,
that one innocent smile,
could turn into this.
Far beyond euphoria,
running towards the unknown.
Ready for the day,
our love becomes a home.

TRINITY

Because you are my first true love,
My second,
And lastly my present.
Wrapped perfectly in bow ties,
And
Calculated written phrases.
Words that only we speak.
Consumed in your presence,
You are the gift I have long awaited for,
Christmas Eve,
in true fashion.
I've played this out in my mind.
I am Eve and you must be Adam,
Our limbs remain bare.
A love consuming between lifetimes,
like Revelations to Genesis.
You are the beginning of where my selfishness ends.
I am learning love,
while you cradle me.
A love, reborn,
this is evident every time I smile.
When I hear you say to me,
my baby.

POETRY IN MOTION

Colors rearranged,
Dancing in the sky.
Coral pinks and electric blues,
nothing more beautiful.
Each color holds its respective space.
Waiting for the perfect time to stand out.

I close my eyes to listen.
Waves clashing,
feet patter,
against the sand.
Rippling waves moving in sequence,
closing in on the shore.

In stillness,
clarity, peace, and love,
re-energize my spirit.
Today, this is what I'm most thankful for.

BUDDING

Embracing changes.
Whether people leave or stay.
Shedding and rebuilding,
patience, my go to trait.
Defining who I am,
moving at my own pace.
Comfortable with the extra space.
I'm right where I need to be,
This is God's work,
It is not a race.
I'm growing daily,
in his grace.

UNPAID DEBTS

I retraced all my steps.
I went back to apologize to each one.
I still felt incomplete.
Because I had one more apology left,
Me.
I owed it to myself.
I faced myself, and pleaded,
please forgive me.

MATCH POINT

I've done the internal and external work.
This love is unmatched.
All the time I was waiting for someone else,
when I was the ultimate catch.

LOVE OUT LOUD

Let me be the first to say,
I love you.
Just so you don't have to wonder.

FINALLY

Finally.
I feel as beautiful,
inside as I feel outside.
Finally.
I feel free enough to embrace my imperfections,
I stressed about way too often.
Finally.
It feels good to love me just for me.
Convinced I am enough,
I've set me free.

DID YOU ENJOY THIS BOOK?

I sure hope so!

Please join our family and write a review. Reviews are the "tip jar" of the book publishing industry. New readers weigh reviews heavily in deciding to make a purchase. Your being so generous as to share your experience is the lifeblood of the success of "Returning to Love."

Much Love, Londyn

ACKNOWLEDGEMENTS

Donald and Anita you set the foundation of unconditional love. I'll forever stand on it. Mommy and Daddy for always letting me bloom freely. Toy a lifetime of thank you's for never ever letting me feel alone. My savior in human form. Jasmine loving me when I felt unlovable and your constant encouragement. Tiffany your wisdom and insight hand in hand along my ups and downs. Kim my editor for your patience and support throughout my writing and always an ear to listen to my crazy ideas and bringing them to life. To all those I've had an opportunity to give and receive love from, you inspire me. Thank you. Most importantly God who's taught me love is an immeasurable gift.

ABOUT THE AUTHOR

Londyn Michaele is a poet and writer from the Midwest. She uses her online platform, through written works and visual storytelling. She focuses on the storytelling of self-love, self-healing, as a reflection of love in the various stages of any relationship. Inspired by her own personal relationnships, her work unfolds through its own beautiful journey whether it is love starting or love ending. She aims to support, uplift, and encourage those who are walking their own pathways and discovering the unknowns of love for themselves.

Made in the USA
Coppell, TX
08 January 2021